W9-CEV-588

Bullard Sanford
Memorial Library
520 W. Huron Ave.
Vassar, MI 48768

Archaeology

Excavating Our Past

THE STUDY OF SCIENCE

Archaeology

Excavating Our Past

Edited by Heather Moore Niver

Britannica®
Educational Publishing

IN ASSOCIATION WITH

ROSEN
EDUCATIONAL SERVICES

Published in 2015 by Britannica Educational Publishing (a trademark of Encyclopædia Britannica, Inc.) in association with The Rosen Publishing Group, Inc.
29 East 21st Street, New York, NY 10010

Copyright © 2015 by Encyclopædia Britannica, Inc. Britannica, Encyclopædia Britannica, and the Thistle logo are registered trademarks of Encyclopædia Britannica, Inc. All rights reserved.

Rosen Publishing materials copyright © 2015 The Rosen Publishing Group, Inc. All rights reserved.

Distributed exclusively by Rosen Publishing.
To see additional Britannica Educational Publishing titles, go to rosenpublishing.com.

First Edition

Britannica Educational Publishing
J.E. Luebering: Director, Core Reference Group
Anthony L. Green: Editor, Compton's by Britannica

Rosen Publishing
Hope Lourie Killcoyne: Executive Editor
Heather Moore Niver: Editor
Nelson Sá: Art Director
Nicole Russo: Designer
Cindy Reiman: Photography Manager
Karen Huang: Photo Researcher
Introduction and supplementary material by Judy Monroe Peterson.

Library of Congress Cataloging-in-Publication Data

Archaeology: excavating our past/edited by Heather Moore Niver.—First edition.
        pages cm.—(The study of science)
Includes bibliographical references and index.
ISBN 978-1-62275-403-8 (library bound)
1. Archaeology—Juvenile literature. 2. Civilization, Ancient—Juvenile literature. I. Niver, Heather Moore.
CC171.A76 2014
930.1—dc23
                                                                2014004694

Manufactured in the United States of America

On the cover: *Marques/Shutterstock.com; cover and interior pages borders and backgrounds © iStockphoto.com/ LuMaxArt*

CONTENTS

Archaeologists mapping their finds at Pachacamac, Peru, an indigenous town occupied from approximately 200 BCE to 1532 CE, when it was sacked by conquistadors under the command of Francisco Pizarro. © AP Images

Everyone, young and old, has a natural curiosity about past civilizations, human cultures, and how ancient people once lived their daily lives. Popular movies, television shows, and books provide fictional adventure stories of the discovery of strange ancient cities with unusual characteristics. Archaeology tells the real story of how humans evolved and cultures developed. Archaeological research is important because it is the main method used to learn about societies that existed before writing was invented. It also provides additional knowledge about ancient civilizations that left written records.

The word *archaeology* was first used in 1837. The term is made up of two Greek words— *archaios*, meaning "ancient" or "old," and *logia*, meaning "learning" or "study." At that time, most archaeologists studied ancient things. By the mid-20th century, archaeological research had expanded to include finding out how and why cultures change.

Archaeologists use scientific methods and analytical technologies to answer questions about humankind's past. They carefully locate and study artifacts, or the remains of things fashioned by people. Artifacts include habitation structures, tools, clothing, pottery,

weapons, jewelry, and art. Other materials, such as the bones of animals that were eaten and residual plant materials that were grown or collected for food, are also examined. Based on their discoveries, archeologists piece together the knowledge of when, where, and how ancient people once lived.

A place where evidence is found becomes an archaeological site. At a site, a team of archaeologists follows a series of standard-ized steps to recover, study, and report on the artifacts made and used by ancient people. It is equally as important that plant and ani-mal foods eaten or discarded be recovered, if available.

To accomplish a successful recovery, sci-entists first identify, map, photograph, and evaluate the area. Once an area is targeted for excavation, they divide the surface of the site into a grid pattern of squares. Locations where artifacts are found are recorded on the grid map, which helps the team determine where to look for additional artifacts. Archaeologists use computers to document each recovered object. They also measure and record the position and depth of each artifact and take photographs or videos to capture recovery details for future research.

Some artifacts and other materials from the sites are studied in laboratories. To interpret the evidence, archaeologists classify, or group the objects, often by shape. Next, they date them. A widely used dating method is radiocarbon dating, which requires organic material, such as shells, bones, and plant parts. The scientists then evaluate the objects to learn how and where they were made and used. Finally, they publish their findings in government and university reports and scientific journals. Some findings are also presented in articles written for the general public.

The work of archaeologists is invaluable, because it explains and protects the past. The more people know about their past, the more they understand how they are connected with each other and the environment of long ago. This knowledge also helps show how people can successfully interconnect with the environment today and in the future.

CHAPTER 1

BRANCHES AND TRAINING

The field of study called archaeology combines the excitement of treasure hunting with the investigative labor of detective work. The materials of archaeological study are both the things made by people and the things used by them. All the things fashioned by people—including settlements, buildings, tools, weapons, objects of ornament, and pure art—are called artifacts. Nonartifactual materials—things that were used but not made or fashioned—include the unworked bones of the animals that were eaten, the traces of the plants that were either grown or collected for food, and the charcoal from ancient hearths.

Since the mid-20th century there has been another shift in the emphasis of archaeological study: from finding out how cultures change to trying to understand why they change. Some modern archaeologists are trying to establish archaeology as a true science from which generalizations or laws can be made about the causes of cultural change.

Archaeologists put artifacts, such as these swords and armor from the 1700s, into historical context to help us better understand the past. DEA/G. Dagli Orti/ Getty Images

TRAINING

Usually a student of archaeology obtains a Bachelor of Arts degree and then pursues a doctorate in a chosen field of archaeology. In addition to classwork, the graduate student must complete work in the field and in the laboratory. The student often uses this work to support a thesis—an original dissertation outlining and supporting the solution of some

ARTIFACTS

In archaeology, artifacts are the material remains of past human life and activities. These include everything from the very earliest stone tools to the human-made objects that are buried or thrown away in the present day: everything made by human beings—from simple tools to complex machines, from the earliest houses, temples, and tombs to palaces, cathedrals, and pyramids.

The main aim of the archaeologist is to place artifacts in historical contexts, to supplement what may be known from written sources, and to increase understanding of the past. Because it concerns things people have made, the most direct findings of archaeology bear on the history of art and technology. By inference archaeology also yields information about the society, religion, and economy of the people who created the artifacts.

specific archaeological problem of the student's choosing. Once students have earned their Ph.D. (Doctor of Philosophy) degrees, they are ready to look for a job in archaeology. Archaeologists are employed in museums, colleges and universities, government agencies, and private research foundations.

BRANCHES

There are two main branches of archaeology: classical, or historical, archaeology and anthropological, or prehistoric, archaeology. The education and training of an archaeologist are divided along these two lines, though the general sequence of each is similar.

CLASSICAL ARCHAEOLOGY

Classical, or historical, archaeology explores the records and artifacts of ancient civilizations. Classical archaeologists are particularly interested in the early cultures of the Mediterranean and the Near East—especially Greece, Rome, Persia (now Iran), Egypt, and Mesopotamia (now part of Iraq)—and also in the civilizations of ancient China, of the Indus River valley in modern Pakistan, and of

15

Southeast Asia. The field of classical archaeology has become prominent in many countries interested in preserving their national heritage.

Naturally the curriculum for classical archaeology includes the basic principles and methods of archaeology. However, it also emphasizes historical studies—including art history and the study of classical civilizations—as well as philology (the study of literature and linguistics), ceramics, architecture, mineralogy, and other subjects.

Graduate students in archaeology complete work in the laboratory as well as in the field, as seen here in an excavation at the Fort Vancouver National Historic Site by students from Portland State University. © AP Images

ANTHROPOLOGICAL ARCHAEOLOGY

Anthropological, or prehistoric, archaeology focuses on prehistory—the time before written records were kept. The curriculum emphasizes such studies as physical and cultural anthropology and linguistics as well as archaeology itself. The anthropological archaeologist is involved in interdisciplinary studies—with particular emphasis on the way such fields as paleontology, human evolution, geomorphology, geology, and aerial photography relate to archaeology and how the archaeologist can use their principles and methods.

CHAPTER 2

HOW ARCHAEOLOGISTS WORK

The great majority of archaeological work involves collecting, analyzing, and synthesizing data. The process of collecting data is divided into two parts: reconnaissance—locating and recording a site and studying the geography of the area—and excavating, or actually digging at the site. Once materials are collected, they are analyzed to determine the time period and the civilization from which they came and to reconstruct the people's way of life. Then the information obtained from this analysis is synthesized, or collected in reports that provide histories, sometimes called cultural-historical integrations.

Most archaeological research ends here. Some archaeologists, however, may go on to analyze the histories themselves in order

Archaeological fieldwork may be carried out by anyone from an individual to a large team of archaeologists. This archaeologist brushes soil from bones in Nebraska.
Tom McHugh/Photo Researchers/Getty Images

to produce hypotheses, or tentative explanations, about why particular cultural changes took place. Then they test those hypotheses against archaeological data to see whether that data supports their hypotheses. If it does, the archaeologists believe they have arrived at a law or generalization that explains the development of the human race and why certain changes took place thousands or even millions of years ago.

THE ARCHAEOLOGICAL TEAM

The size of an archaeological team depends on the financial resources available. Teams range from a solitary digger to the kind of military-like organization that Mortimer Wheeler directed at Mohenjo-daro in Pakistan in the mid-twentieth century.. A team as large and well-funded as the latter may have three branches: administrative, laboratory, and excavational. Under the administrative director or chief are the quartermaster corps, accountants, secretaries, and mechanical and nonskilled staff that keep the whole organization going. The laboratory chief supervises artists, draftsmen, scientific analyzers, repairers, and specimen numberers, as well as computer staff. The excavational, or digging, branch includes various crew chiefs and their assistants, recorders, photographers, artists, and the diggers themselves,

Sir Mortimer Wheeler (1890–1976) was a British archaeologist known for his finds in Great Britain and India as well as for his advancement of scientific method in archaeology. Chris Ware/Hulton Archive/ Getty Images

who are often students. The diggers may work at a variety of jobs or they may specialize in certain jobs such as troweling, screening, or removing dirt or refuse.

MOHENJO-DARO

The largest city of the ancient Indus Valley civilization was Mohenjo-daro, located on the right bank of the Indus River, in what is now southeastern Pakistan. The civilization existed from about 2500 BCE to 1700 BCE on the Indian subcontinent. Today the remains of the city are an archaeological site. It was first excavated in 1922 by Sir John Hubert Marshall and was declared a UNESCO World Heritage site in 1980.

Mohenjo-daro is a remarkable example of ancient urban planning. The city measured about 3 miles (5 kilometers) around. Artificial barriers were built around the city to protect it from the Indus River. Laid out with great precision, Mohenjo-daro was divided into about a dozen blocks, or "islands." Each island was about 1,260 feet (384 meters) from north to south and 750 feet (228 meters) from east to west. At the central block on the western side are the ruins of a citadel, or high fortress, that was built up with mud and mud bricks to a height of 20 to 40 feet (6 to 12 meters). Square towers of baked brick fortified the structure. Buildings on the citadel included an elaborate bath or tank surrounded by a veranda, a large residential structure, a huge granary, and at least two

(continued on the next page)

halls of assembly. The citadel must have been the religious and ceremonial headquarters of Mohenjo-daro.

In the lower town were substantial courtyard houses, indicating that there was a considerable middle class. Most houses had small bathrooms and, like the streets, were well-provided with drains and sanitation. The houses had brick stairs, so they must have had at least an upper story or a flat, habitable roof. The walls were originally plastered with mud.

One of the best-known works of art recovered from Mohenjo-daro is a bronze figure of a young dancing girl wearing several armlets. Not much stone sculpture was found at the site, but there were numerous small sculptures of terra-cotta or clay depicting animals and people. Several seals found at Mohenjo-daro are beautifully carved with patterns of animals such as bulls, elephants, and especially unicorns. The seals carry inscriptions in Indus script.

Seeds of wheat and barley have also been recovered from the ruins, indicating that these crops were grown at Mohenjo-daro. Millet, dates, melons, and other foods, as well as cotton, were also known to the Indus Valley civilization.

It is believed that Mohenjo-daro was attacked and destroyed about the middle of the 2nd millennium BCE. The identity of the attackers is uncertain. The city had already been declining, however, as heavy floods had more than once submerged large areas. Houses had become increasingly shoddy and showed signs of overcrowding.

PRELIMINARY FIELDWORK

The first stage of collecting archaeological data—the discovery and recording of sites and their superficial examination—is called preliminary fieldwork. Many sites have been found by pure luck. The famous 20,000-year-old wall paintings in Lascaux, France, for example, were discovered by boys who climbed into a hole to find their missing dog. Some sites have been uncovered in the course of preparation for

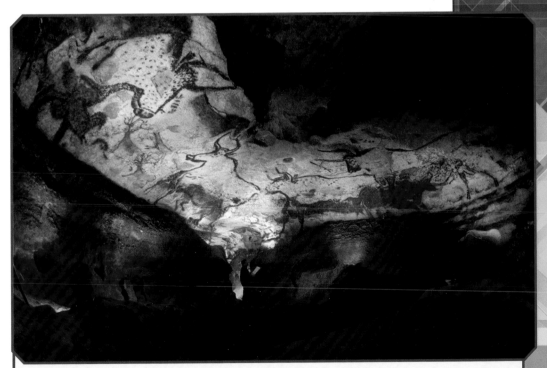

If not for two boys in search of their lost dog in 1940, it may have been years before anyone discovered the prehistoric cave paintings in Lascaux, France. Sissie Brimberg/ National Geographic Image Collection/Getty Images

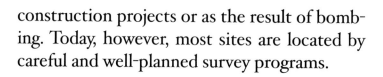

construction projects or as the result of bombing. Today, however, most sites are located by careful and well-planned survey programs.

RECONNAISSANCE TECHNIQUES

The exact methods of finding archaeological sites vary, primarily because there are so many different types of sites. Some sites—such as mounds, temples, forts, roads, and ancient cities—may be easily visible on the surface of the ground. Such sites may be located by

Ancient Inca ruins, Machu Picchu in Peru's Andes Mountains, were discovered almost completely unbroken. In 1983 the ancient city was designated as a UNESCO World Heritage site. Curioşo/Shutterstock.com

simple exploration: by an individual or group going over the ground on foot, in a jeep or car, or on a horse, mule, or camel. This kind of survey can be comprehensive—that is, the entire area may be covered—or it can involve the technique of sampling. In sampling, a limited number of strategic spots in the region are checked for signs of an underlying archaeological site. Sampling was not widely used in the United States until passage of the Archaeological Resources Protection Act of 1979. This act, designed to protect the archaeological heritage of an area, has encouraged archaeological sampling of areas in which archaeological remains might exist that are in danger of being destroyed by construction or by the growth of cities.

To find sites that have no surface traces, archaeologists may use aerial photographs taken from balloons, airplanes, or satellites by cameras with remote sensors, infrared film, or other devices. The archaeologist checks these photographs for clues—such as variations in soil color, ground contour, or crop density—that may indicate the existence of a site.

Archaeologists may simply probe the ground with sound to check for variations in reflection of sound that would indicate

the presence of structures or hollows in the ground. A probe, or periscope, may be inserted into the ground to locate walls and ditches. The archaeologist Carlo Lerici used such a probe, called a Nistri periscope, to locate and photograph Etruscan tombs in Italy in 1957.

Other modern devices use electricity and magnetism to locate buried structures. Electron or proton magnetometers or even mine detectors may be used to force currents through the earth and record any unusual features, such as a large, solid object, that lie beneath the soil. Similar magnetometers are dragged through the water to locate sunken ships or structures. The 20th-century archaeologist George Bass and the explorer Jacques Cousteau both had considerable success using this technique.

Explorer, oceanographer, filmmaker, and inventor Jacques Cousteau (1910–1997). © AP Images

RECONNAISSANCE RECORDS

All survey programs must be properly recorded and the sites designated—that is, given some sort of name or number. The simplest ways of designating a site are to name it after its discoverer, after the owner of the property on which it was found, or after its location. Another simple method is to give the site a serial number: site 1 for first site found, for example, or Fo^{v}1 to mean the first (1) village (^{v}) in Fulton County (Fo). More complex systems of identification may involve grid coordinates such as latitude and longitude, township and range, or geographic blocks.

Although there is no universally accepted system for recording the discovery of a site, most survey records include the site's designation, its exact location, the date it was found, the discoverer, the size of the site, and some sort of description of the site itself and what was found there. Of particular interest are structures such as mounds, temples, and houses and artifacts such as pieces of pottery and stone tools.

CHAPTER 3

EXCAVATION

Perhaps the most important idea for an archaeologist to keep in mind during excavation is that any archaeological digging is, in fact, destroying a nonrenewable resource. Careful excavation and scrupulous record keeping and specimen preservation are therefore critical.

PREPARATION

The first step in excavation is to make a record of the site before it is dug or changed in any way. This preliminary record often involves making a contour map and taking photographs of the site. To make such maps and photographs meaningful, some mechanism must be set up to measure locations on the site. Vertical measurements—depths and heights—are often taken with respect to an agreed-upon base point, called the datum point, and are recorded as so many centimeters below or above the datum. The site may also be

Some archaeological sites are divided into squares, or grids, which gives the archaeologists a way to organize the area and record the locations of their finds. Kathryn Scott Osler/ Denver Post/Getty Images

divided into horizontal units so that the provenience, or original location, of artifacts may be exactly recorded. Often the site is gridded, or staked out into squares. Then a system is devised for designating the location of each unit or square.

Before major digging actually begins, some sort of test is generally performed to determine the best part of the site in which to carry out the main part of the excavation. (Large sites are usually not dug out entirely.) One way to do this is to dig test holes called sondages.

Instead of digging up an entire area, archaeologists dig test holes called sondages, which may be random, be in specific strategic locations, or follow a pattern. Dorling Kindersley/Vetta/Getty Images

These may be spaced throughout the site at random, or they may be dug in certain strategic locations or in a checkerboard pattern. Crosswise, parallel, or crisscross trenches may be dug through the site instead.

DIGGING

Although the stereotypical tool of archaeology is the spade, the archaeologist's real tool is actually the trowel, which is used to scrape, slice, or clean away soil. Other tools of the

DATING

Dating, in geology, involves determining a chronology or calendar of events in the history of the Earth. It makes use of the evidence of organic evolution in the sedimentary rocks accumulated through geologic time in marine and continental environments. To date past events, processes, formations, and fossil organisms, geologists employ a variety of techniques. Some of these techniques establish a relative chronology in which occurrences can be placed in the correct sequence relative to one another or to some known succession of events. Radiometric dating and certain other approaches are used to provide absolute chronologies in terms of years before the present. The two approaches are often complementary, as when a sequence of occurrences in one context can be correlated with an absolute chronology elsewhere.

trade include spoons, picks, paintbrushes, and dissecting needles.

There are a wide range of excavational techniques, and the method that an archaeologist uses depends very much on the type of the archaeological site. Usually the dirt is removed by stripping off horizontal layers to expose the artifacts and other materials. The layers may be of an arbitrary thickness or they may correspond to natural strata, or layers of sedimentary rock or earth. Sometimes excavation is done vertically by slicing down through the different strata. Sometimes a combination of both techniques is used. The excavator must scrupulously record and preserve all archaeological materials as they are uncovered.

RECORD KEEPING

Archaeologists use various methods for recording data from a dig. Traditionally, they have made field notes and kept diaries describing what was being done and what was found. These records were generally accompanied by maps and drawings to show both the

Even underwater archaeologists need to keep notes on their work. Their notes may be accompanied by maps, drawings, and photographs. © AP Images

horizontal units dug from the site, called floor plots, and the vertical units, called cross sections, and indicating the artifacts and other materials found in them. Photographs or films might also accompany these records. Other methods for recording specific data include square-description forms, diary forms, soil forms, pollen forms, and similar kinds of recording aids. In the mid- to late 20th century, archaeological recording has increasingly been done using computers, digitizing cameras, and various other advanced devices.

If an archaeological specimen is not too fragile, it might simply be stored in a plastic bag with a label and a number. Danny Daniels/Stockbyte/Getty Images

PRESERVATION

As with most other steps in the excavation process, the methods used for preserving archaeological specimens depend on the nature of the site. A less delicate specimen may be placed in a bag with a label and number. In some cases artifacts are coated with preservative chemicals. The advances in technology and chemistry made since the 1950s have enabled archaeologists to perform remarkable feats of preservation that would probably have been impossible a few decades ago.

CHAPTER 4

INTERPRETING ARCHAEOLOGICAL FINDS

Ideally, analysis of the materials found on a site begins in the field laboratories while excavation is still in progress. Often, however, reconnaissance and excavation are completed in a relatively brief period of time, and the records and preserved remains are taken back to a museum, university, or laboratory for more analysis. This analysis has many aspects, which include describing and classifying objects by form and use, determining the materials from which they were made, dating the objects, and placing them in environmental and cultural contexts. These aspects may be grouped into two broad categories: chronological analysis and contextual analysis.

CHRONOLOGICAL ANALYSIS

Chronological analysis of archaeological materials—identifying their time periods and sequence in time—is often done first. Archaeologists use two general kinds of dating methods: relative dating, or

establishing when the various materials found at a site were made or used in relation to each other, and absolute dating, or assigning a fairly precise, chronometric date to a find.

RELATIVE DATING

The oldest method of establishing relative dates is by analyzing stratigraphy—the arrangement of strata in a site. This technique is based on the assumption that the oldest archaeological remains occur in the deepest strata of the excavation, the next oldest in the next deepest strata, and so on. By following this assumption, archaeologists can place the materials collected from the various strata into a rough chronological sequence.

If archaeologists digging in an undated site find a distinctive type of pottery for which the date is known, they may conclude that the other materials found in the site along with the pottery bear the same date as the pottery. This is an example of a relative-dating technique called cross dating.

Similarly, archaeologists may assign a date to an artifact based on the geologic region or strata with which the artifact is associated. For example, archaeologists may conclude that hand axes found in the high terrace of the Thames River in

England are older than arrow points and pottery found in the lower terrace because they know that the high terrace was formed earlier than the low one. The association of artifacts with animal or fossil remains can also be used for relative dating. For example, it is known that superbison became extinct in the Great Plains of what is now

Relative dating helped archaeologists realize that the modern bison (shown here) was preceded by the now-extinct superbison. RRuntsch/Shutterstock.com

the United States and were replaced by modern bison. Thus if archaeologists discover one site in which Folsom fluted points (the distinctive tips of a kind of prehistoric human-made weapon) are found imbedded in superbison remains, and they discover a second site in which a different kind of points, called Bajada points, are sticking in the remains of modern bison, they may conclude that Folsom points were made before Bajada points. This kind of relative dating may also be done using plant remains, particularly plant pollen, which is often preserved in archaeological strata.

If archaeologists know how certain types of artifacts—styles of pottery or burial objects, for example—evolved over time, they may be able to arrange groups of these artifacts in chronological order simply by comparing them. This method is called seriation.

Archaeologists can judge the relative dates of bones by analyzing their fluorine content, since the amount of fluorine in buried bones increases over time. In the 1840s Dr. Montroville Dickeson proved that a human pelvis found in Natchez, Miss., dated from the same time as mammoth bones found with it because both had accumulated the same proportions of fluorine.

Because fluorine amounts increase in bones the longer they are buried, scientists can compare bones, like this mammoth pelvis, to determine whether or not they are from the same time period. Robyn Beck/AFP/Getty Images

There are many other methods of relative dating. None of them is as accurate as the absolute-dating methods, however, because the assumptions on which many relative-dating techniques are based can be misleading. Nevertheless, sometimes relative dating is the only method available to the archaeologist.

ABSOLUTE DATING

In absolute, or chronometric, dating, a definite age—in numbers of years before the present—is assigned to an archaeological specimen. When applied correctly, the methods of absolute dating can yield highly accurate dates. The remains found by classical archaeologists—coins or written records, for example—may have dates already written on them, but this is not always the case. It is never the case for anthropological archaeologists, who study prehistoric materials.

Mud and clay deposited into lakes by glaciers sink at different speeds and form noticeable layers called varves. Scientists can determine dates for the artifacts or sites related to each varve. George Whitely/Photo Researchers/Getty Images

One system of absolute dating, called varve dating, was developed in the early 20th century by Gerard de Geer, a Swedish geologist. He noted that the mud and clay deposited by glaciers into nearby lakes sank to the lake bottom at different rates throughout the year, forming distinct layers, called varves, on the lake bottom. Because each year's layer was different, the researchers were able to establish dates for artifacts or sites associated with a specific varve.

A similar absolute-dating method—dendrochronology, or the dating of trees by counting their annual growth rings—was first developed for archaeological purposes in the early 1900s by the American astronomer Andrew Ellicott Douglass. If an ancient structure has wooden parts, archaeologists can compare the number and widths of the growth rings in those parts with sequences from other samples to find out when that structure was built. Other techniques yield absolute dates based on the thickness of the patina, or residue, that forms over time on certain stone artifacts.

Advances in the physical sciences during the 20th century greatly improved absolute-dating methods. One of the best-known and most valuable techniques is radiocarbon dating (also called radioactive carbon dating, carbon dating, and carbon-14 dating). All living things

ARCHAEOASTRONOMY

Archaeoastronomy (also known as historical astronomy and astro-archaeology) focuses on the role that astronomical phenomena have played in ancient societies. Some of the disciplines that make up archaeoastronomy are geology, anthropology, mythology, folklore, philology, paleography, ethnology, prehistoric art studies, prehistoric and classical scholarship, biology, botany, geochemistry, and nuclear physics.

Archaeoastronomy includes both applied and ceremonial aspects of astronomy. The origin of calendars, navigation systems, and the astronomical alignment of ancient architecture (the Egyptian pyramids, Stonehenge, Mayan structures) are examples of applied astronomy. The role of constellations in the formation of mythologies is an example of ceremonial astronomy.

Sir Joseph Norman Lockyer (1836–1920) is generally recognized as the Father of Archaeoastronomy for his works *The Dawn of Astronomy* (1894) and *Stonehenge and Other British Stone Monuments* (1906). The field gained popularity in the 1960s through the work of U.S. astronomer Gerald Hawkins's studies of lunar alignments at Stonehenge and Scottish astronomer Alexander Thom's work on the geometry of English stone circles.

In studying preliterate cultures, archaeoastronomy can help determine the purpose of various artifacts, such as the megalith Stonehenge: its alignment suggests that its builders were interested in the position of the sun in relation to the passage of the seasons. In studying postliterate cultures, such astronomical observations as the alignment of the Governor's Palace at Uxmal, Mexico, to the southernmost rising point of Venus can be used in conjunction with the Venus glyphs (drawings) adorning the palace to gain insights into the ancient Mayan world view.

contain small amounts of carbon-14, a radioactive form of carbon. After death, this carbon-14 changes, or decays, into a more stable form of carbon. Archaeologists can determine the age of once-living things such as bones, wood, and ash by measuring the amount of carbon-14 remaining in the specimen.

Radiocarbon dating cannot be used to make accurate age measurements of very old materials—materials more than about 70,000 to 100,000 years old. For such objects, archaeologists can use similar techniques involving other chemical elements. Potassium-argon dating, for example, can be used to date rocks millions of years old. A related dating method called fission-track dating can be used on certain stone samples of almost unlimited age. Another modern dating method, thermoluminescence dating, can be used to find out when ancient pieces of pottery or other fired-clay objects were made.

CONTEXTUAL ANALYSIS

Determining the chronology of an artifact is only half of the archaeologist's task; the other half is reconstructing the ancient culture from which the artifact came. This process is called contextual analysis.

The lowest, or most basic, level of contextual analysis consists of analyzing a culture's systems of subsistence and technology—that is, the ways in which ancient people adapted to their environment. The next level involves reconstructing their social structures and settlement patterns. Finally, archaeologists try to reconstruct a culture's ethos, or guiding beliefs.

Each of these levels requires different analytical methods. Archaeologists may start reconstructing an ancient subsistence system by determining what the people ate. They may do this through coprology, the examination of fossilized feces, or by analyzing human bones for the presence of certain forms of carbon and nitrogen. The study of the plant remains found in a dig can also provide clues to a people's diet.

By studying ancient tools—such as arrow tips, butcher knives, and grinding stones—archaeologists can find out how people obtained and prepared their foods. Archaeologists may also be able to determine how ancient people made and used their tools. Studying the work of a modern flint knapper, for instance, may show an archaeologist how ancient people made flint tools. (In archaeology, this type of

Ancient tools such as this axe blade can teach archaeologists a lot about how people got and prepared their food. The Bridgeman Art Library/Getty Images

reasoning or interpretation is called ethnographic analogy.)

When archaeologists attempt to reconstruct ancient social structures, they often use data gathered by ethnographers, social anthropologists, and historians. The excavated materials themselves may also provide hints of ancient social organization. Specialized

Statues, such as these excavated terra-cotta warriors from ancient China, can help archaeologists piece together the belief systems of ancient people. Neale Cousland/ Shutterstock.com

artifacts that are found concentrated in certain areas may indicate that the ancient culture had full-time craft specialists, and different types of burial arrangements may indicate that social classes existed.

Reconstructing the highest level of a culture, including its values, ethos, or religion, is the most difficult type of contextual analysis. Such items as statues or paintings of figures that appear to be supernatural, buildings that may have been temples, and evidence of religious ceremonies can all be used to help reconstruct ancient systems of beliefs.

The goal of chronological and contextual analysis is to write and publish records of ancient history. Excavated materials have value only if the information gained from them is disseminated through books, magazines, and other publications. Such publications not only keep track of how techniques have changed but also record great archaeological discoveries.

CHAPTER 5

HISTORY OF ARCHAEOLOGY

Like any history, the development of archaeology may be divided into stages. To some degree these periods reflect changing interests and objectives as well as changing techniques in archaeology. The stages are also marked by great finds and famous names.

THE FIRST ARCHAEOLOGISTS: BEFORE 1860

The interests and objectives of the first archaeologists are the most difficult to define. Perhaps they acted more out of curiosity than for any well-defined, scholarly goal. In the Old World, a landmark event in early archaeology was the removal of ancient Greek sculptures, now known as the Elgin Marbles, from their site in Athens, Greece, to England from 1803 to 1812. This acquisition, which was arranged by the English diplomat and art collector Thomas Bruce,

This section of the Elgin Marbles in ancient Greece was part of a larger sculpture collection that Thomas Bruce, 7th earl of Elgin, had moved to England in 1803. Graham Barclay/ Getty Images

7th earl of Elgin, aroused violent controversy, and Bruce was widely denounced as a vandal.

By 1812 a national museum of archaeology had already been established in Denmark. By 1818 its curator, Christian J. Thomsen, had developed the three-part chronological system that divides human prehistory in Europe into the Stone, Bronze, and Iron ages. Thomsen was assisted by Jens Worsaae, whose subsequent discovery of ancient human

remains established the Paleolithic as a period of prehistory.

In 1837 the French archaeologist Jacques Boucher de Crèvecoeur de Perthes discovered Stone Age tools and other remains in France. He was the first to draw scientific attention to evidence that humankind had lived on Earth much earlier than had been previously thought. The English archaeologist Austen Henry Layard was responsible for two milestones in early archaeology. During the 1840s he excavated Calah, the capital of Assyria under King Ashurnasirpal II, and Nineveh, the oldest and most populous city of the ancient Assyrian Empire and its capital for hundreds of years. At both sites Layard discovered the remains of palaces, including the palace of the Assyrian King Sennacherib, and a large number of significant artworks. Perhaps most important, however, was his discovery of many cuneiform tablets from the state archives, from which much about Assyrian and Babylonian culture and history was learned. Other archaeological milestones were the translation of the Rosetta stone by French scholar Jean-François Champollion and Henry Rawlinson's translation of the cuneiform inscriptions on the Bisitun rock. These translations provided the key to deciphering the writings of ancient Egypt and Mesopotamia, respectively.

Thomas Jefferson had some burial mounds excavated to see if Native Americans had built them. Science Source

In the New World the Father of American Archaeology, Thomas Jefferson, excavated burial mounds in Virginia in the early 1790s to determine if the mound builders were Native Americans. Other early American research included the mapping of Mayan ruins by the

51

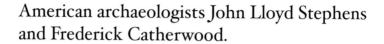

American archaeologists John Lloyd Stephens and Frederick Catherwood.

WELCOMING THE PALEOLITHIC: 1861–1901

With the rise of Darwinism and the theory of evolution, archaeology underwent a momentous change. During the second half of the 19th century the idea of the Paleolithic evolved—a period in the Stone Age that represented

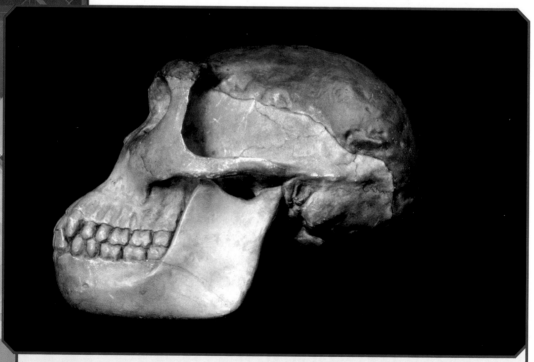

Java man's fossil remains were found on the island of Java, Indonesia. These bones were the first known fossils of the species Homo erectus. E.R. Degginger/Photo Researchers/Getty Images

a stage, or level, of human development characterized by the use of rudimentary chipped-stone tools. The French archaeologist Gabriel de Mortillet refined the concept by subdividing the Paleolithic into six subperiods. Archaeological evidence of human physical evolution included specimens of such human ancestors as Java man (discovered in 1891–92) and Neanderthal man (1856). In 1879 magnificent Paleolithic wall paintings were discovered in the Altamira caverns in Spain.

Inspired by these Old World finds, American anthropologists Frederic Putnam, William John McGee, and others began a search for evidence of Paleolithic man in the New World. A more immediate concern of most American archaeologists, however, was determining who built the mysterious ancient mounds in the Midwest United States. Archaeologists who studied the mounds included Clarence Moore, Warren Moorehead, Stephen Peet, and Charles Willoughby.

In the Mediterranean other archaeologists excavated classical sites. In the early 1870s the German archaeologist Heinrich Schliemann began exploring the ruins of ancient Troy. The British archaeologist and Egyptologist Flinders Petrie conducted numerous valuable

Arthur Evans spent a year digging on the island of Crete before he uncovered the ruins of the palace and the city of Knossos, as well as evidence of a splendid, complex ancient civilization. Trevor Creighton/Lonely Planet Images/Getty Images

excavations in Egypt beginning in the 1880s, including explorations of the Great Pyramid at Giza and the Temple of Tanis.

Beginning in the late 1890s the British archaeologist Arthur Evans excavated the ruins of the ancient city of Knossos in Crete and uncovered evidence of a sophisticated Bronze Age civilization, which he named Minoan. Art treasures from historic and pre-historic archaeological sites flowed into the museums of Europe and the United States.

NEW THEORIES: 1901–32

In the New World in the early 20th century, the field of anthropology came to be dominated by the theories of the German-born anthropologist Franz Boas. His view that different human groups developed in different ways not because of genetic differences but because of differences in their environmental, cultural, and historical

CARLETON COON

U.S. anthropologist Carleton Coon (1904–81) made notable contributions to cultural and physical anthropology and archaeology. His areas of study ranged from prehistoric agrarian communities to contemporary tribal societies in the Middle East, Patagonia, and the hill country of India.

Carleton Stevens Coon was born on June 23, 1904, in Wakefield, Mass. He earned a Ph.D. from Harvard University in 1928 and taught there from 1927 to 1948. During World War II he served with the Office of Strategic Services in Africa. In 1948 he joined the faculty of the University of Pennsylvania and became curator of ethnology at the university's museum, serving in the two positions until 1963.

Coon is perhaps best remembered for his general works *The Story of Man* (1954) and *The Seven Caves* (1957), a history of archaeology in the Middle East. His other books include *Caravan* (1951), *The Origin of Races* (1962), and *The Hunting Peoples* (1971). He died on June 6, 1981, in Gloucester, Mass.

55

circumstances changed the theories and practices of his colleagues not only in anthropology but also in other fields, including archaeology.

Under the direction of anthropologist Fay-Cooper Cole, the University of Chicago established its now-famous school for archaeological fieldwork, and teams from the university excavated mounds and sites in Fulton County, Ill. Frank Roberts's discovery of Folsom fluted points alongside extinct bison bones in Folsom, N.M., firmly established that humans had been living in the Americas for as long as 10,000 years.

In Europe studies of the Paleolithic progressed as more human fossil remains were uncovered. Danish and British archaeologists established the existence of Mesolithic culture, and the Australian-born British archaeologist Vere Gordon Childe began his famous studies of Neolithic cultures in the region of the Danube River.

For European classical archaeology this was the era of the great expeditions. The British archaeologist Leonard Woolley conducted his famous excavation of the ancient Sumerian city of Ur in present-day Iraq and made many valuable archaeological finds; the French archaeologist Jean-Vincent Scheil headed an expedition to the site of Susa in present-day

Folsom fluted points were found along with the bones of extinct bison, proving to Frank Roberts that humans had been in North America for up to 10,000 years. Tom McHugh/Photo Researchers/Getty Images

Iran and uncovered, among other objects, the Code of Hammurabi—the most complete existing collection of Babylonian laws; and the British archaeologist Howard Carter found a magnificent treasure in the unlooted tomb of King Tutankhamen in Egypt.

Archaeologists also studied remains of the high cultures of the New World—the Aztecs, Maya, and Incas. George Vaillant undertook excavations of ancient sites and cities in the

Valley of Mexico; Sylvanus Morley started work on Mayan sites in the Yucatán Peninsula; and Max Uhle and other archaeologists explored the great sites of Peru.

ARCHAEOLOGY AND THE DEPRESSION: 1932–62

It is ironic that in the United States the Great Depression did more to advance archaeology than did any other single event. As part of his program to employ American citizens,

President Franklin D. Roosevelt set up the Works Progress Administration, which helped save archaeological sites that would be covered by water as a result of the Tennessee Valley Authority project. © AP Images

President Franklin D. Roosevelt established the Works Progress Administration and set up a government-sponsored archaeological program to rescue archaeological sites that would be covered by water in the Tennessee Valley Authority project.

In South America the basic chronologies of ancient cultures were established by Wendell Bennett, Junius Bird, and J.C. Tello in Peru; by Irvin Rouse in the Caribbean; and by J.M. Cruxent in Venezuela. In Mexico and Central America, Alfred Vincent Kidder continued Sylvanus Morley's investigation of Mayan sites on the Yucatán Peninsula and in Honduras and Guatemala. George Vaillant, Paul Tolstoy, and others continued reconstructing chronologies in the Valley of Mexico. In Palenque, Mexico, Alberto Ruz opened the tomb in the Mayan Temple of Inscriptions. Richard MacNeish and Paul Mangelsdorf began their long search for the origins of corn agriculture, the basis of subsistence of Meso-American cultures.

World War II followed close on the heels of the Great Depression, and in the Old World achievements in prehistoric archaeology declined considerably. The British archaeologists Graham Clark and Vere Gordon Childe dominated the field of Mesolithic and Neolithic studies. Paleolithic studies flourished worldwide with the work of François

Bordes and Hal Movius in Europe; Mary and Louis Leakey in Africa; Davidson Black in China; and Robert Braidwood and Dorothy Garrod in the Middle East.

Developments in classical archaeology continued, though also on a reduced scale. Among the most notable events were Kathleen Kenyon's excavation of Jericho to its Stone Age foundations, the discovery of the Dead Sea Scrolls, and the deciphering of Mycenaean script by Michael Ventris. Underwater archaeology began during this period, and various technological improvements—satellite photography, radiocarbon dating, the use of computers and metal detectors to locate sites and to record data—aided archaeological efforts.

One of the most pressing challenges for modern archaeology is preventing the destruction of archaeological sites, which results in the loss of data and the knowledge it provides. With the cooperation of governmental authorities, archaeologists hope to find a way of stopping such destruction and of preserving the traces of humankind's ancient history.

CHAPTER 6

RECENT TRENDS AND DISCOVERIES

In the second half of the 20th century there was an emphasis on theory in archaeology—particularly dealing with the question of why cultures change. Other trends in modern archaeology included an increasing reliance on computers and other technological advances and a tendency toward well-planned interdisciplinary programs designed to answer specific archaeological questions.

Archaeology in the United States was greatly affected by passage of the Archaeological Resources Protection Act and by the Environmental Protection Agency's establishment of cultural resource management programs. These measures required that, before any government-sponsored project begins, archaeologists search the area affected for any possible archaeological sites that might be destroyed. If such sites are found, the government required that they be excavated or protected to preserve any data.

The period produced some sensational finds. They included the discovery in Ethiopia of a 3-million-year-old skeleton called Lucy, regarded by many as belonging to an early humanlike species; the discovery of the tomb of Philip II of Macedon, father of Alexander the Great, in northern Greece; and the discovery in northern Guatemala of Nakbe, the earliest-known Mayan center.

Major finds in the late 1980s included the unearthing in Oklahoma of stone tools that might be evidence of the earliest groups of

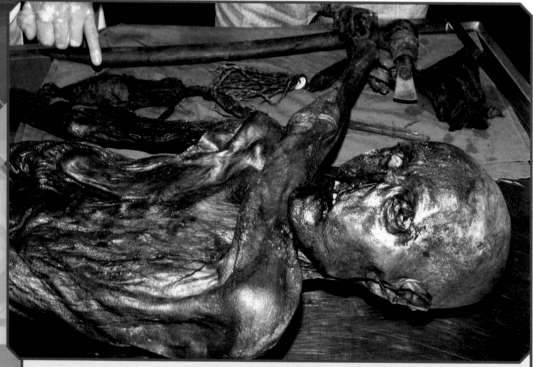

Although the body of the Iceman is thought to be from more than 5,000 years ago, its skin, internal organs, and fingernails are all intact. It still had clothes, shoes, and weapons. AFP/Getty Images

humans to inhabit North America; the discovery in Iraq of the world's oldest statue, an 11,000-year-old stone in the shape of a human; and the discovery in London of the remains of Shakespeare's Globe Theatre. A virtually intact body of a man from the late Stone Age was discovered in the Austrian Alps in 1991. The body was so well preserved it still had its skin, internal organs, and fingernails, as well as its clothes, shoes, and weapons. Dubbed the Iceman from the Similaun, the body is believed to be at least 5,000 years old.

In February 1996 a team of United Nations–sponsored archaeologists announced that they had discovered the ancient birth chamber of Prince Siddhartha Gautama, the founder of Buddhism, beneath the Mayadevi temple in southwestern Nepal. The site, which was located in Lumbini, more than 200 miles (350 kilometers) southwest of the Nepalese capital, Kathmandu, appeared to settle an international debate over whether Buddha was born in India or Nepal.

A team of American and Russian archaeologists announced the findings they recorded during the lengthy excavation of a series of ancient tombs that date back to the 6th century BCE, which were discovered along the westernmost border of Kazakhstan. Most surprising

among the findings were the contents found within tombs of females. The women had been buried along with swords, daggers, bows, and arrows, leading many of the archaeologists to the preliminary conclusion that at least some of the female members of Sauromatian and Sarmation nomadic tribes, to which the tombs had been traced, served as warriors. One of the most provocative graves was that of a bowlegged young woman who had been buried with a dagger and a quiver containing 40 bronze-tipped arrows. The woman's bowed legs, combined with the armaments at her side, seemed to indicate that she was trained both in horseback riding and archery and was perhaps skilled in the practice of mounted warfare. Some observers suggested that the women warriors bore some relation to the mythical Amazons, powerful female warriors of whom the Greek historian Herodotus had written. Archaeologists involved with the excavation stated that any connection between the entombed women and the legendary Amazons was largely speculative.

For more than two and a half centuries, the final resting place of one of history's most notorious sea vessels remained a mystery. In 1718 *Queen Anne's Revenge*, which had been the fleet flagship of the infamous pirate Edward

Pirate Blackbeard (Edward Teach, or Thatch). Hulton Archive/Getty Images

Teach, was sunk off the Atlantic coast of the American colonies. Teach, known popularly as Blackbeard, escaped from the sinking vessel along with his crew. Legend has it that they

were able to save the vast treasures they had accumulated during two years of plundering ships and towns along the Eastern seaboard.

Although the whereabouts of the rumored treasure remained unknown, marine archaeologists working off the coast of North Carolina discovered what they believed to be the sunken remains of the *Queen Anne's Revenge*. The hull of the ship apparently settled near where it was reported to have sunk, in water little more than 20 feet (6 meters) deep and less than 2 miles (3.2 kilometers) from the coast. The location of the ship had remained undetermined for more than 270 years mostly because of the clutter of other ships at the bottom of the ocean in that area. Since the time of the ship's sinking, literally hundreds of ships had come to rest in the vicinity of the suspected resting place of the *Queen Anne's Revenge*. The team of marine archaeologists, however, consulted a rare book from 1719 that chronicled the story of the sinking of Blackbeard's notorious ship, which ran ashore in 1718 while attempting to enter Beaufort inlet near North Carolina. The book provided an exact description of the location where the ship went down, and the marine archaeologists were able to locate the *Queen Anne's Revenge* using that information and a sophisticated device designed to detect

The infamous pirate Blackbeard's ship, the Queen Anne's Revenge, *sank and was not located until 1976, when a special device detected the metal from the ship's many cannons.* © AP Images

large amounts of metal. This device made it possible for the archaeologists to detect the ship's numerous cannons.

In November 1996, after a decade-long process of research and underwater searching, the team of marine archaeologists finally located the hull of a ship that seemed consistent with known information concerning the design of the *Queen Anne's Revenge*. It was only after a team of divers salvaged several artifacts

from the hull, including the bell of the ship, that they were able to conclude that the ship in question was most likely Blackbeard's legendary vessel. (The bell had been inscribed with the date 1709, the year that construction was believed to have been completed on the *Queen Anne's Revenge*.) Marine archaeologists continued excavating at the site and eventually were able to confirm that the ship was the *Queen Anne's Revenge*. They recovered a large number of artifacts, including glass bottles, pottery fragments, and utensils, as well as two anchors, more than one dozen cannons, and some 250,000 pieces of lead shot. Two cannons retrieved in 2013 each weighed about 1 ton (0.9 metric ton).

NAUTICAL ARCHAEOLOGY

A team of marine archaeologists led by Robert Ballard, an internationally renowned scientist who made headlines when he located the remains of the ocean liner *Titanic* in 1986, announced in 1997 yet another extraordinary discovery made in the depths of one of the world's most well-traveled bodies of water, the Mediterranean Sea. Using a sophisticated nuclear submarine on loan from the United States Navy, the marine archaeologists located

Oceanographer and marine biologist Robert Ballard used innovative technologies for his underwater explorations that led to the discovery of, among other things, the Titanic. John B. Carnett/Popular Science/Getty Images

five ships in the depths of the Mediterranean that had sunk over a period of 2,000 years. Three of the wrecks were relatively modern. One, believed to be a relic of the Ottoman Empire, dated back to the 18th or 19th century. Two more ships, believed to be of European origin, also dated back to the 19th century, the archaeologists estimated. Two other ships

discovered at the bottom of the sea, however, were believed to have originated in the classical world, when the imperial powers of Rome and Carthage dominated the region and its shipping routes. One of the ships, a Roman shipping vessel, was believed to be a cargo ship that sank in the rough waters of the Mediterranean in the beginning of the 1st century BCE. The other ship, also a Roman shipping vessel, dated to the 1st century CE. Archaeologists lauded the research team for their extraordinary effort in actually recovering numerous priceless objects from the two Roman vessels, and historians unanimously praised the discovery as one that would redefine modern perceptions of trade in the ancient world.

Since the earliest days of human civilization on the Levant and on the Southern European and North African coasts, the Mediterranean Sea had served as the main overseas artery of trade for several empires, such as the Greek, the Phoenician, the Egyptian, and the Sumerian. Historians have never doubted the seafaring acumen or the trading instincts of these early civilizations; on the contrary, these empires were renowned for their far-flung trading empires. Historians did, however, long believe that trade between these overseas empires was largely confined to coastal routes along the Mediterranean until the advent of more sophisticated navigational tools, such as the compass in the 12th century, allowed seamen to venture further from the safety of the shores. This untested hypothesis remained largely unchallenged until recent times, primarily because underwater archaeological techniques remained too crude to probe much further than several hundred feet underwater—hardly deep enough to uncover whatever treasures might rest at the bottom of the Mediterranean, with its average depth of 9,000 feet (2,700 meters) below sea level.

In 1989, however, a research team led by Robert Ballard made a discovery that began a radical alteration of conceptions of seafaring and trading in the classical world. In that year the research team, using a deep-sea robotic probe, discovered the remnants of a 4th century CE vessel that the team dubbed *Isis*. In the hull of the Roman ship the researchers found amphorae—clay containers used to ship and store goods—and other trading items that led the researchers to conclude that the downed ship had been used to transport goods for trade. The location of the wreck, which was discovered off the eastern coast of the island of Sicily, led the archaeologists to conclude that the trading ship had been en route to the area of modern Tunisia, which

Deep-sea robotic probes investigate underwater using remote control. They can explore the ocean floor far below the surface of the ocean. Kyodo/AP Images

at the time was the capital of the Carthaginian empire. There is (and was) no land route between the Sicilian island and the Carthaginian capital, so the trading vessel had probably set out with the intention of crossing the open sea.

The 1989 discovery prompted the archaeologists to set their sights on a stretch of the sea lying more than 100 miles (160 kilometers) to the northwest of Sicily, in the dangerous 2,500-foot- (760-meter-) deep waters of the Mediterranean that lay between Sicily and the island of Sardinia. The archaeologists borrowed a United States Navy NR-1 nuclear submarine to probe the depths of the sea in search of other wrecks. Using long-range sonar and the same robotic underwater probe that had allowed the archaeologists to locate the *Isis*, Ballard's team ultimately discovered a trail of debris that led them to the downed wreckage of five ships within a 20-square-mile (52-square-kilometer) region—the discovery that Ballard announced in 1997. The two Roman sea vessels they found seemed to confirm Ballard's speculation about the seafaring abilities of the Roman traders.

The two ships, each roughly 100 feet (30 meters) long, contained numerous objects that indicated that the two vessels were indeed trading ships. While both of the vessels underwent significant decomposition during their many centuries under the sea, those sections of the ships that were embedded in the ocean floor remained well preserved. The hulls of both ships remained largely intact, and both were filled with a wealth of objects. Using the robotic deep-water probe, the archaeologists

recovered more than 100 items from the two ships. The older ship contained glass artifacts similar to kitchenware, as well as numerous amphorae that once carried perishable goods such as wine and oil to foreign lands. Inside the second vessel the archaeologists found cargo that, while arguably more significant, was too bulky and heavy to retrieve. Contained in the hull of the second ship were slabs of granite and pieces of columns apparently bound for some section of the Roman Empire or neighboring lands. The granite and columns enclosed in the ship's hull led the archaeologists to speculate that the second ship might well have contained a prefabricated temple, to be constructed at the point of destination.

Given the magnitude of their discovery, the archaeologists involved in the first deep-sea probe of the Mediterranean seemed justified in their optimistic belief that their newfound underwater surveying technique would revolutionize the fields of marine archaeology and ancient history. The new technique would allow archaeologists to look for more wreckage on the Mediterranean floor, which given its average depth, must contain a tremendous amount of antiquity. It is likely that future discoveries will rewrite the economic history of the Roman world.

ROBERT BALLARD

At two o'clock in the morning on September 1, 1985, in the North Atlantic some 560 miles (900 kilometers) south of Newfoundland, the United States Navy research ship *Knorr* slowly cruised the dark swells. About 13,000 feet (4,000 meters) beneath the *Knorr*, tethered to it by a thick steel cable and skimming the ocean bottom in icy darkness, was a 16-foot (5-meter) submersible robot sled christened *Argo*. Suddenly *Argo*'s video cameras, working in the glare of searchlights, sent to television screens aboard the *Knorr* images of the greatest shipwreck of all time. Resting upright on the edge of a submarine canyon, shorn of its stern and two of its four smokestacks yet otherwise beautifully preserved after 73 years, lay the ocean liner *Titanic*. Robert Ballard's search was over.

As head of the Deep Submergence Laboratory of the Woods Hole (Mass.) Oceanographic Institution, Ballard designed *Argo* and was in charge of testing it for the Navy. He chose the *Titanic* as his goal because it had sunk in a depth ideal for testing the deep-sea explorer. Teaming up with the French vessel *Le Suroit*, which until late June conducted its search for the ocean liner by towing an unmanned submersible equipped with side-scanning sonar for mapping the ocean bottom, the *Knorr* began combing the site of the disaster in early August. After *Argo*'s cameras picked up pictures of a large riveted metal cylinder (a *Titanic* boiler), the *Titanic* was located by the *Knorr*'s 25-year-old sonar system. *Argo* and an older Woods Hole sled, *Angus*, snapped 12,000 color photos. Mission accomplished, Ballard and his team returned home to worldwide acclaim.

(continued on the next page)

Robert Duane Ballard was born in Wichita, Kan., on June 30, 1942. In 1966, a year after graduating with a degree in chemistry and geology from the University of California at Santa Barbara, he joined the United States Navy and was assigned as liaison officer for the Office of Naval Research at Woods Hole. He became a civilian researcher there three years later, at first working with *Alvin*, a three-man submersible. From 1973 to 1975 he dived 9,000 feet (2,750 meters) in *Alvin* and in a French submersible to explore the Mid-Atlantic Ridge. In 1976 he took *Alvin* 12,000 feet (3,660 meters) down into the Cayman Trench in the Caribbean, and in 1977 and 1979 he joined an international team exploring hydrothermal vents in the Galápagos Rift and the East Pacific Rise.

ANCIENT RUINS DISCOVERED IN CAMBODIAN JUNGLE

A team of archaeologists studying the ancient Khmer civilization of Cambodia announced in 1998 that they had discovered a series of previously unknown Khmer temples and a human-made mound in the jungle of northwestern Cambodia. The newly discovered temples predate by as much as 300 years the nearby temple of Angkor Wat—a well-known and magnificent Hindu temple constructed by the Khmer people in the middle of the 12th century CE.

The newfound archaeological structures were first detected during a space shuttle mission conducted by the National Aeronautics and Space Administration (NASA) in 1994. In December 1996, NASA, working in coordination with archaeologist and Khmer civilization expert Elizabeth Moore of the University of London, surveyed the densely vegetated region using advanced microwave radar imaging. The radar images produced enough evidence to suggest that some sort of human-made structure existed deep beneath the thick foliage. In December of 1997, Moore led a team of archaeologists through the Cambodian jungle in search of the structures depicted in the radar surveys. Traveling carefully through regions controlled by guerrilla armies, the archaeologists eventually discovered the remains of six additional temples in the area near Angkor Wat, as well as a human-made mound that was built as early as the 6th century BCE. The newly discovered ruins were estimated to have been built at some point in the late 9th or early 10th century CE.

The discovery of the new temples profoundly changed archaeological conceptions

of the Khmer civilization and the ancient Khmer city of Angkor. At the height of its power, the city of Angkor was believed to have spanned 100 square miles (260 square kilometers) and to have been inhabited by as many as 1 million people. More than 1,000 temples were believed to have been built in Angkor. In the 15th century the city was mysteriously abandoned, and the jungles slowly encroached on the ancient city, burying the ruins beneath a thick carpet of vegetation. Western scholars first became familiar with the ancient city of Angkor during the middle of the 19th century, after the area then known as Indochina was claimed as a colony by France. In the beginning of the 20th century, French archaeologists began excavating the massive temple of Angkor Wat, which was believed to have been built in the mid-12th century. Archaeological accounts of the early excavation recorded only one other temple near Angkor Wat, and no structures were known to have existed from before the 12th century. Moore stated that the discovery of the six temple ruins, as well as the human-made mound, indicated that the region was probably regularly inhabited for much of the 1,000 years preceding the construction of Angkor Wat.

UNLOCKING MORE STONEHENGE SECRETS

The prehistoric monument known as Stonehenge includes a circular arrangement of massive, upright stones surrounded by a large circular earthen embankment. It was built between about 3100 and 1500 BCE and is located about 8 miles (13 kilometers) northwest of Salisbury, in southern England. There are hundreds of similar structures throughout

Archaeologists continue studying the prehistoric Stonehenge in Wiltshire, England, hoping to understand the significance behind its structure. Justin Black/ Shutterstock.com

Britain. Stonehenge and the nearby circular monument called Avebury were designated as UNESCO World Heritage sites in 1986.

Stonehenge is believed to have been a place of worship of some kind. Many explanations have been offered as to why the enormous monument was built, including speculations that it was a type of astronomical clock for predicting eclipses or a temple for sky worship. These ideas have never been proven, however, and the specific reasons for its construction remain unknown. An earlier notion connected Stonehenge to the Druids, a caste of Celtic priests, but it is now known that the monument was built long before Druids reached the area.

In 2010, archaeologists who were studying Stonehenge found evidence of yet another ring less than 1 mile (1.6 kilometers) away, but this one was constructed of wood. A circular trench surrounds another loop of 24 pits that would have allowed wooden posts to support a free-standing structure as high as 10 feet (3 meters). This makes it a comparable size to Stonehenge. Archaeologists estimate that the structure, known as "Woodhenge," was built around 4,500 years ago, in the Neolithic period, but who built it and why still remains a mystery.

TECHNOLOGICAL ADVANCEMENTS REVOLUTIONIZING ARCHAEOLOGY

Technological advancements in the 21st century are revolutionizing all scientific fields, including archaeology. The continual improvement of computing speed and ease of data storage, retrieval, and manipulation has provided archaeologists with new tools for reconnaissance, excavation, and interpretation of archaeological finds.

The first objective of archaeology is to locate and record potential places where human activity occurred. Using lidar (light detection and ranging) technology, scientists can accurately measure the earth's surface topography. Lidar is remote-sensing equipment that shoots laser beams and analyzes the reflected light to compute precise distances. When lidar is applied to the Earth from an airplane, a computer generates a detailed, three-dimensional, contour model of the land. Archaeologists then study the contours to quickly find ancient human structures, such as burial mounds, buildings, and building foundations. They can clearly

identify the land topography even when trees, bushes, and other vegetation densely cover it.

The most important task at an excavation is to determine the date of its human use. The site often provides organic artifacts and materials, such as wood, bone, shell, or charcoal. Carbon dating of organic material has been the standard technology since the 1950s. This method is accurate and has given archaeologists much information about humankind's existence. However, carbon dating requires a large mass of 9 to 10 grams (0.3–0.4 ounces) of organic materials, which is converted to charcoal for analysis. Such conversion can severely damage or even destroy artifacts. Today, archaeologists use accelerator mass spectrometry (AMS) carbon dating for more efficient radiocarbon dating. Artifacts are not harmed using this process because only an extremely small sample (about one ten-thousandth the size of a carbon-dating sample) is necessary for analysis.

The absolute dating of an archaeological site is a primary fact that archaeologists require to determine what human culture inhabited an area and how the artifacts were used. Organic artifacts can be dated using a wide variety of carbon dating techniques. To date inorganic material, such as pottery or soil buried with organic artifacts, archaeologists can use a technique called optically stimulated luminescence. The technique measures the amount of electrons that have been trapped over time in the crystalline structure of certain minerals, such as the quartz found in grains of sand. In OSL, a light illuminates a tiny sample of the mineral, which in turn, emits a small amount of light that can be measured to determine its accumulation of electrons. The technique can measure when a piece of pottery was fired in a kiln or when a sample of buried soil was last exposed to the sun.

One example of the application of OSL was to study tiny quartz grains recovered at a Paleo-Indian siltstone manufacturing site in northern Minnesota. By using this process, researchers found new information about the ice glacier that retreated from the area 12,500 years ago and how humans existed during that time period.

Archaeology, like all sciences, is evolving into a multidisciplinary process. Biology, geology, chemistry, physics, mathematics, and electronic computing are deeply interconnected with every phase of the archaeological search for information about humankind. By applying new technologies, archaeologists continue to increase the world's knowledge and facts about ancient peoples.

CONCLUSION

Archaeology is the scientific study of mankind's past based on finding and analyzing both artifacts and natural objects. It is the main method for learning about prehistoric and historic cultures. Archaeologists reconstruct the lives of ancient people, including their technology, societies, religions, and economies. Based on their research, they

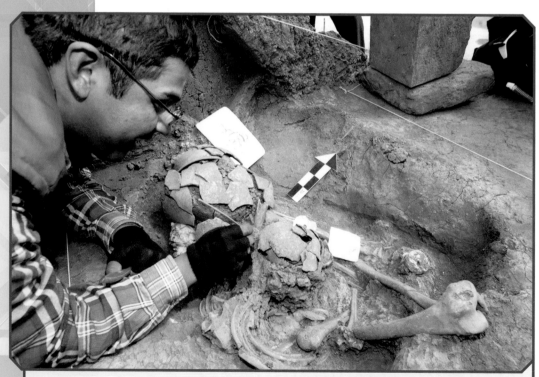

An archaeologist in Tiwanaku, Bolivia, works carefully to clean the bones of a young male found with the bones of a llama, some gold, and various vessels. Aizar Raldes/ AFP/Getty Images

develop generalizations, or laws, about how societies evolve.

The materials of archaeological study are the physical remains of past human activity. Archaeologists often have to work with fragments from past lives. They use the tools of chronological and contextual archaeology to produce and publish accurate records of ancient human history. These publications also provide information on the application of new and continually changing technologies. Archaeologists usually have advanced degrees and are experts in many different scientific fields.

Archaeology fascinates people because it focuses on finding out why cultures change. It draws on many other disciplines to answer questions about human origins and development. This knowledge leads to a deeper understanding of how people live today and how they will connect with their future environment.

GLOSSARY

absolute dating A method that uses physical or chemical analysis to determine the specific date of an artifact or site.

AMS (atomic mass spectrometry) A method carried out at an atomic level that measures the amount of radioactive carbon-14 decay in organic materials to determine their age.

archaeology The scientific study of the remains of peoples from the past to understand how they lived.

artifact An object made by people.

chronological analysis The identification of a time period and sequence in time when an object was used by people.

contextual analysis The identification and reconstruction of the human culture from which an artifact came.

coprology The study of fossilized feces.

cross dating A method that dates a site by comparing an excavated artifact with artifacts of another site that have a precise date.

cultural-historical integration The history of a culture based on the analysis of artifacts and materials from an excavation.

datum point An exact geographical location from which all project measurements are compared.

dendrochronology The precise dating of trees by counting their annual growth rings.

excavation The removal of soil to access and collect artifacts and organic materials made or used at a site that was inhabited by people.

flint knapping An ancient method of making flaked stone tools.

lidar (light detection and ranging) A technology that uses a laser beam applied from an airplane to determine a precise three-dimensional land contour.

magnetometer An instrument used to detect the presence of a metallic object.

OSL (optically stimulated luminescence) A method that uses weak emissions of light from a common mineral, such as quartz in sand, to determine the age of buried soils or fired pottery.

potassium-argon dating An absolute dating method used to analyze minerals and elements in rocks that are millions of years old.

provenience The precise location where an artifact was recovered.

radiocarbon dating A method that measures the amount of radioactive carbon-14 decay in organic materials to determine their age.

reconnaissance The location and study of a geographical site prior to excavation.

relative dating A method that dates an object by comparing it to known artifacts found at a site that were made or used in relation to each other.

seriation The chronological ordering of artifacts based on styles arranged into groups by identifying specific characteristics.

sondage A test hole dug at a specific site prior to comprehensive excavation.

stratigraphy The analysis of soil levels and artifacts to understand how a site was inhabited over a period of time.

typology The classification of artifacts based on their similar and different characteristics. In archaeology, this can be the ranking of objects based on age beginning with the oldest object.

FOR MORE INFORMATION

American Anthropological Association
2300 Clarendon Boulevard, Suite 1301
Arlington, VA 22201
(703) 528-1902
Website: http://www.aaanet.org
The American Anthropological Association
    (AAA) is the largest organization in
    the world for people interested in
    anthropology.

Archaeological Conservancy
1717 Girard Boulevard NE
Albuquerque, NM 87106
(505) 266-1540
Website: http://www
    .archaeologicalconservancy.org
Founded in 1980, the Archaeological
    Conservancy is the only nonprofit
    organization in the United States. It
    endeavors to obtain and preserve the
    best enduring archaeological sites in
    the country.

Archaeological Institute of America
Located at Boston University
656 Beacon Street, 6th Floor

Boston, MA 02215-2006

(617) 353-9361

Website: http://www.archaeological.org

Email: aia@aia.bu.edu

The Archaeological Institute of America
(AIA) endeavors to provide support to
archaeologists and their research. It also
seeks to educate everyone "about the significance of archaeological discovery and
advocates the preservation of the world's
archaeological heritage."

Canadian Archaeological Association

189 Peter Street

Thunder Bay, ON P7A 5H8

Canada

(807) 345-2733

Email: president@canadianarchaeology.com

Website: http://canadianarchaeology.com/caa

Founded in 1968, the Canadian
Archaeological Association is open
to professional, avocational, and student archaeologists from any country
who share the goals of the CAA. The
CAA strives to promote the practice of
archaeology and share archaeological
information, especially that relating to
Canada and its surroundings.

Ontario Archaeological Society
P.O. Box 62066
Victoria Terrace Post Office
Toronto, ON M4A 2W1
Canada
(416) 406-5959
Website: http://www.ontarioarchaeology.on.ca
The Ontario Archaeological Society was
    started in 1950. It continues to strive to
    encourage "the ethical practice of archaeol-
    ogy" in the face of destruction by various
    forms of development.

Society for American Archaeology
900 Second Street NE #12
Washington, DC 20002-3557
(202) 789-8200
Website: http://www.saa.org
Email: public_edu@saa.org
The Society for American Archaeology devel-
    ops "understanding and appreciation of
    humanity's past" through archaeological
    investigation. Their site includes educa-
    tional resources, handy links, information
    for educators, and more fun suggestions,
    such as movies, books, and games.

Society for Historical Archaeology
13017 Wisteria Drive #395

Germantown, MD 20874

(301) 972-9684

Website: http://www.sha.org

Email: hq@sha.org

The Society for Historical Archaeology (SHA) focuses on modern-world archaeology, particularly the era since the commencement of European exploration. The society's main focus is on "identification, excavation, interpretation, and conservation of sites and materials on land and underwater."

WEBSITES

Because of the changing nature of Internet links, Rosen Publishing has developed an online list of websites related to the subject of this book. This site is updated regularly. Please use this link to access the list:

http://www.rosenlinks.com/SCI/Arch

Aronson, Marc, and Michael Parker Pearson. *If Stones Could Speak: Unlocking the Secrets of Stonehenge*. Washington, D.C.: National Geographic, 2010.

Berger, Lee, and Marc Aronson. *The Skull in the Rock*. Washington, DC: National Geographic Children's Books, 2012.

Croy, Anita. *Exploring the Past*. New York, NY: Benchmark Books, 2010.

Farndon, John. *Archaeology*. Great Bardfield, Essex: Miles Kelly, 2009.

Ferguson Publishing. *Archaeology* (Careers in Focus). New York, NY: Ferguson, 2010.

Forbes, Scott. *How to Be a Dinosaur Hunter*. Oakland, CA: Lonely Planet, 2013.

Ganeri, Anita, and David West. *The Curse of King Tut's Tomb and Other Ancient Discoveries*. New York, NY: Rosen Publishing, 2011.

Henderson, Harry. *The Leakey Family: Unearthing Human Ancestors*. New York, NY: Chelsea House, 2012.

LIFE Editors. *LIFE Titanic: The Tragedy That Shook the World*. New York, NY: LIFE BOOKS, 2009.

Macdonald, Fiona. *Amazing Archaeologists: True Stories of Astounding Archaeological*

Discoveries. Chicago, IL: Heinemann-Raintree, 2014.

Peterson, Judy Monroe. *Digging Up History: Archaeologists*. New York, NY: Rosen Publishing, 2009.

Rubalcaba, Jill. *Every Bone Tells a Story*. Watertown, MA: Charlesbridge, 2010.

Thomas, William David. *Archaeologist* (Cool Careers). New York, NY: Gareth Stevens Publishing, 2009.

Yount, Lisa. *Robert Ballard: Explorer and Undersea Archaeologist*. New York, NY: Chelsea House, 2009.